PIANO • VOCAL • GUITAR

T0066156

ISBN 978-1-4950-5878-3

Disney characters and artwork © Disney

Walt Disney Music Company
Wonderland Music Company, Inc.

DISTRIBUTED BY

7777 W. BLUEMOUND RD. P.O. BOX 13819 MILWAUKEE, WI 53213

In Australia Contact:
Hal Leonard Australia Pty. Ltd.
4 Lentara Court, Cheltenham, Victoria, 3192 Australia
Email: ausadmin@halleonard.com.au

Visit Hal Leonard Online at **www.halleonard.com**

CALL OF THE GUARD
(The Lion Guard Theme)

Words and Music by
CHRISTOPHER WILLIS

Moderately, in 2

Yo! ma - ma____ ma kum -

be kum - be we, Yo! ma - ma - ma twim - be twim - be, Ma - ma kum - be?

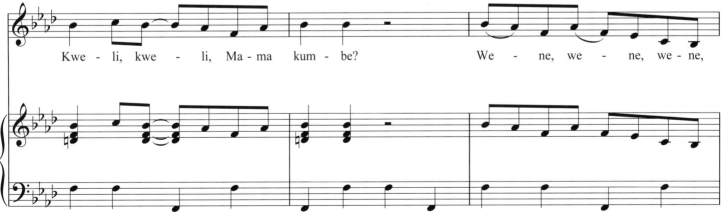

Kwe - li, kwe - li, Ma - ma kum - be? We - ne, we - ne, we - ne,

*Recorded a step higher.

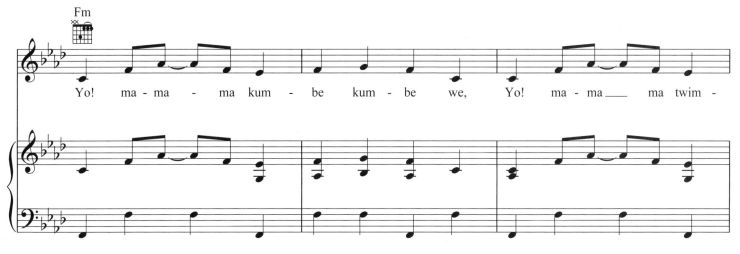

Yo! ma - ma - ma kum - be kum - be we, Yo! ma - ma___ ma twim -

be twim - be, Tu - ta za - me, za - me, za - me! Tu - ta

za - me, za - me, za - me, na - ma la la Wa - la - ki - ki na - na!

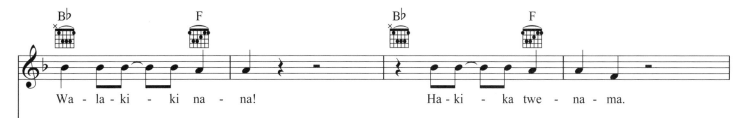

Wa - la - ki - ki na - na! Ha - ki - ka twe - na - ma.

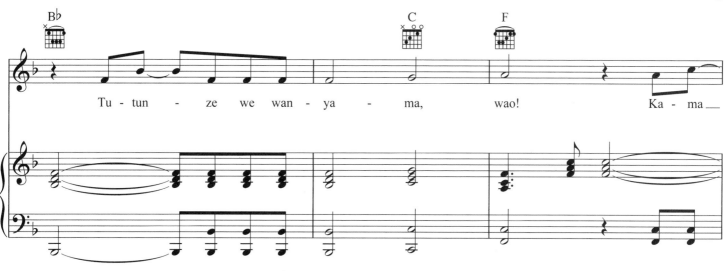

Tu - tun - ze we wan - ya - ma, wao! Ka - ma __

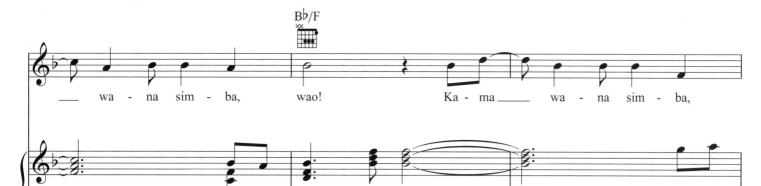

__ wa - na sim - ba, wao! Ka - ma __ wa - na sim - ba,

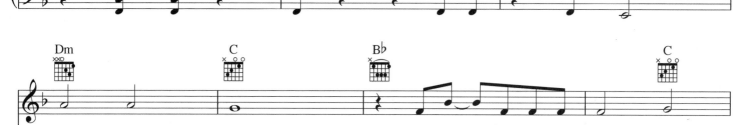

U - un ga na Wan - ya - ma we wan - ya - ma.

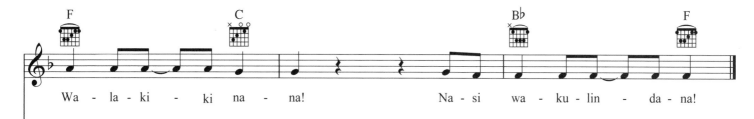

Wa - la - ki - ki na - na! Na - si wa - ku - lin - da - na!

A BEAUTIFUL DAY
(Ni Siku Nzuri)

Words and Music by BEAU BLACK,
SARAH MIRZA and FORD RILEY

Moderately fast, in 2

It's a good day __ to have __ some fun, to run and play. The

*Recorded a half step lower.

sun's so hot, it melts my wor-ries all a - way.

I'm gon - na

take it eas - y, got no rea-son to work all day.

Oh, I'm gon - na

keep on smil - ing, keep on rid - ing all the way.

Come on __ and I'll tell __ ya.

(Ni si - ku n - je - ma ma - ta - ta __ ya - ko mba - li.

Ni si - ku n - je - ma kim - bi - a __ na fu - ra - hi.)

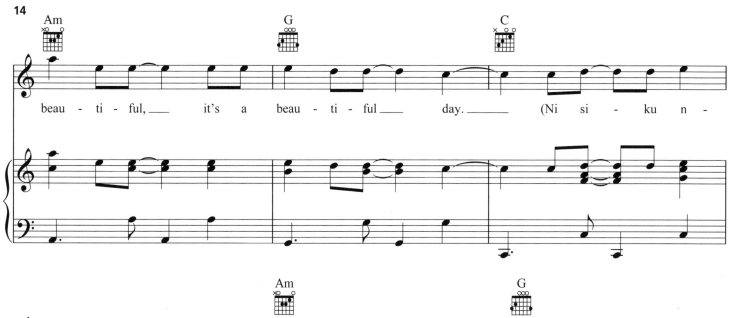

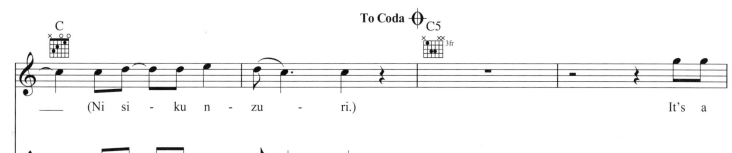

Come play with me, and we'll run free, __

through the pride __ lands up to the high - est tree.

Got - ta live __ for fun, it's the on - ly way. __ It's a

beau - ti - ful, __ it's a beau - ti - ful __ day. __ (Ni si - ku n -

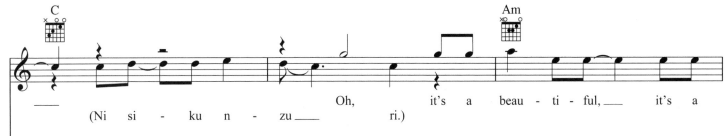

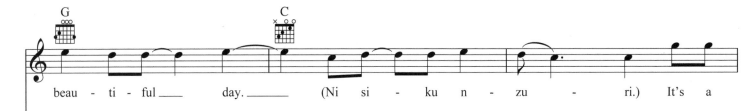

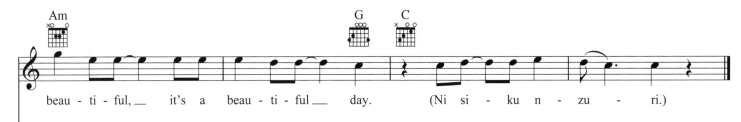

ZUKA ZAMA

Words and Music by BEAU BLACK,
SARAH MIRZA and FORD RILEY

BUNGA: Zu-ka za-ma, zum ___ zum zum! Zu-ka za-ma, zum ___ zum zum!

Life's ex-cit-ing, life is fun

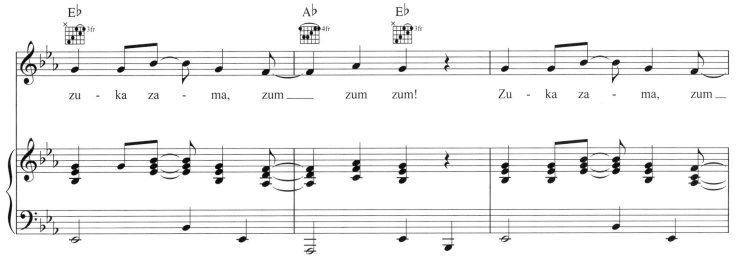

zu - ka za - ma, zum ____ zum zum! Zu - ka za - ma, zum ____

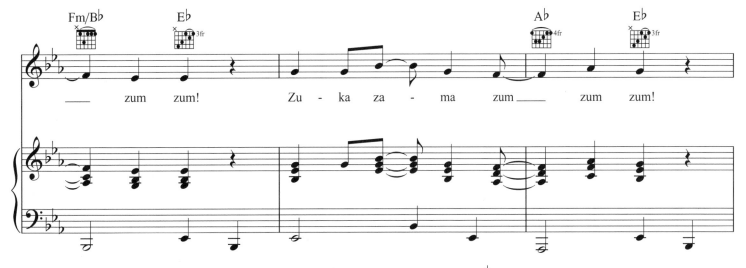

____ zum zum! Zu - ka za - ma zum ____ zum zum!

Zu - ka za - ma, zum ____ zum zum. Now you know ___ my lit - tle

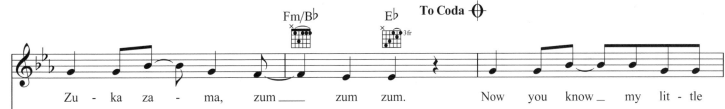

mot - to for life (Zu - ka za - ma, zum ____ zum zum!): en -

CODA

Pop up, pop ___ up (zu - ka zu - ka),

dive in, dive ___ in (za - ma za - ma), go, go, go

(zum zum zum), like a bee, like a bee, like a bus - y bus - y bee, go - in',

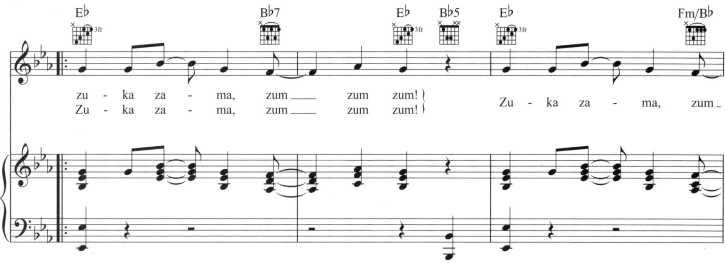

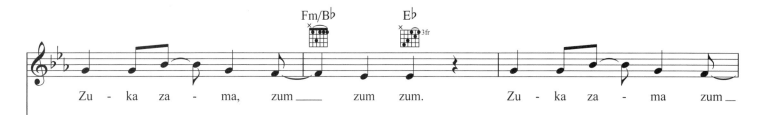

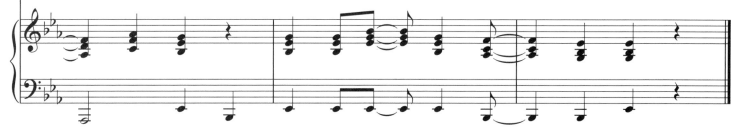

TONIGHT WE STRIKE

Words and Music by BEAU BLACK
and FORD RILEY

Recorded a half step lower.

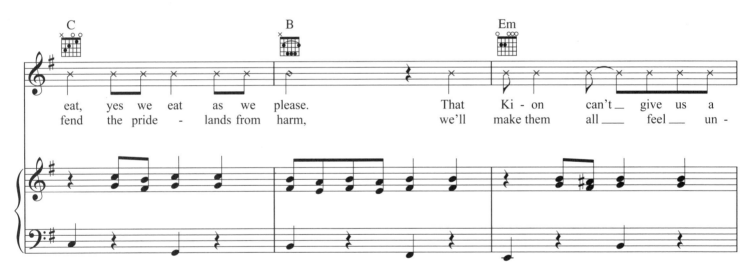

night we strike, to - night we strike. No one's safe, so the

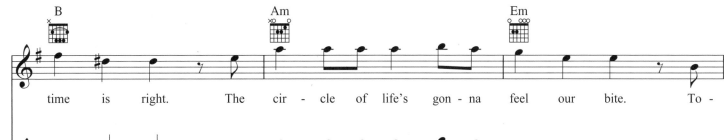

time is right. The cir - cle of life's gon - na feel our bite. To -

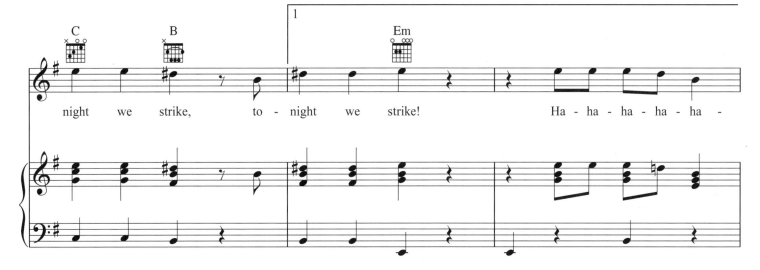

night we strike, to - night we strike! Ha - ha - ha - ha - ha -

ah - ah._____ (Ha - ha - ha - ha - ha - ah - ah._____

JANJA: So be -

neath. And just like a roar - ing thun - der, we'll

wake them up ___ with our teeth!

JANJA, MZINGO & HYENAS:

To - night we strike, to -

night we strike. No one's safe, so the time is right. The

cir - cle of life's gon - na feel our bite. To - night we strike, to -

KION'S LAMENT

Words and Music by BEAU BLACK,
FORD RILEY and CHRISTOPHER WILLIS

KION (Spoken): Dad wanted the best for the Lion Guard. And I found them.

But now...maybe the best isn't good enough? I just don't understand.

Why?   Why e-ven trust___ me at all?___

* Recorded a whole step lower.

34

Expressively

out to be... _____   Kion...

MUFASA *(Spoken):*   **KION:** *Heyvi Kabisa...   Are you...?*

MUFASA: *Yes, Kion. I am your Grandfather.*   **KION:** *Mufasa. I've heard a lot about you.*

MUFASA:
And I've been watching you.   *You are about to embark on a great journey, Kion.*

Leader of the Lion Guard! **KION:** *I'm not sure Dad's gonna let me lead the Lion Guard.   He's worried that I can't handle it.*

Trust your instincts.

The Roar will be there for you when you need it.

And so will I.

Until the Pride Lands' end.

KION: *Grandfather Mufasa?...*

Don't go yet!

Trust my instincts.   The Roar will be there when I need it...

Tempo I, steadily

May-be my jour-ney   is   far   from done.

They need a lead-er,   and

HERE COMES THE LION GUARD

Words and Music by BEAU BLACK,
SARAH MIRZA and FORD RILEY

big at times, _ you feel like you may be fall - ing. If you be-lieve in

who you are __ there's no need to go run - ning: you found your place, _ and

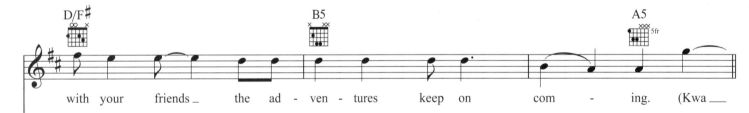

with your friends _ the ad - ven - tures keep on com - ing. (Kwa __

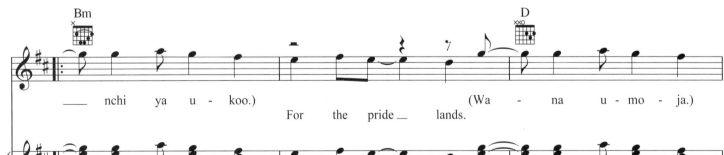

__ nchi ya u - koo.) (Wa - na u - mo - ja.)
For the pride _ lands.

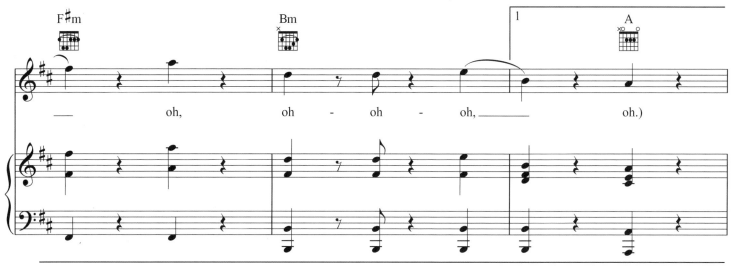

oh, oh - oh - oh, _____ oh.)

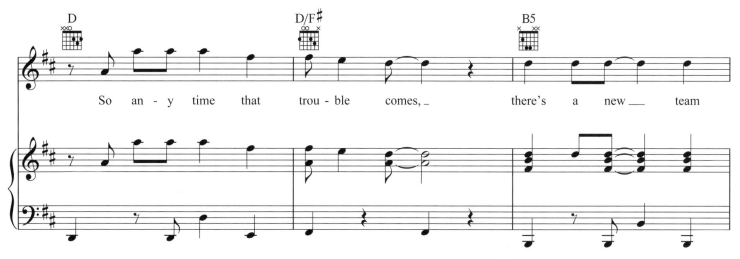

So an - y time that trou - ble comes, _ there's a new _ team

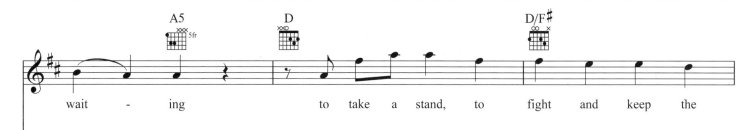

wait - ing to take a stand, to fight and keep the

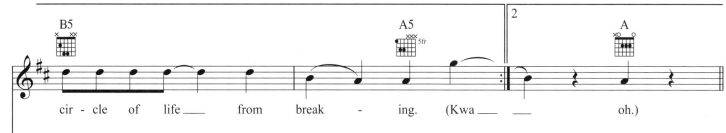

cir - cle of life _ from break - ing. (Kwa _ _ oh.)

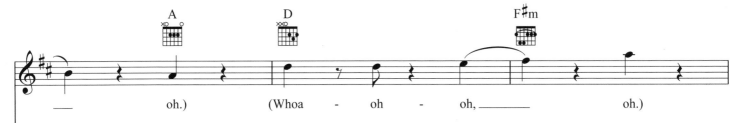

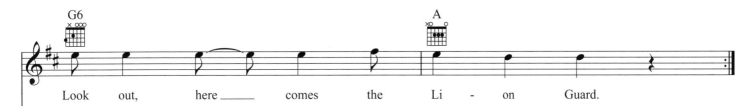

WE'RE THE SAME
(Sisi Ni Sawa)

Words and Music by BEAU BLACK,
KEVIN HOPPS, SARAH MIRZA
and FORD RILEY

JASIRI: You got-ta look past what you see,
'Cause we both know a high-er call,
(2.) (Si - si ni sa - wa.)

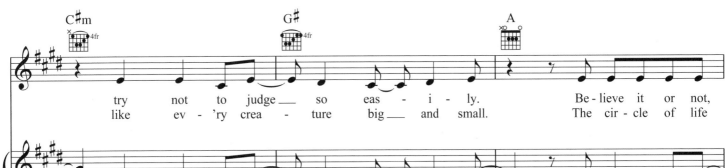

try not to judge so eas-i-ly. Be-lieve it or not,
like ev-'ry crea-ture big and small. The cir-cle of life

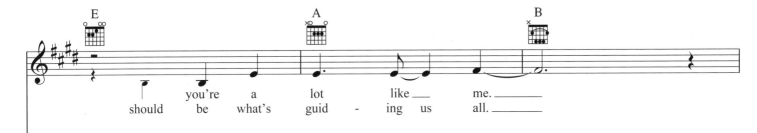

you're a lot like me.
should be what's guid-ing us all.

Said be-lieve it or not, you're a lot like me.
The cir-cle of life will guide us all!

Si - si ___ ni sa - wa: we are the ___ same. ___

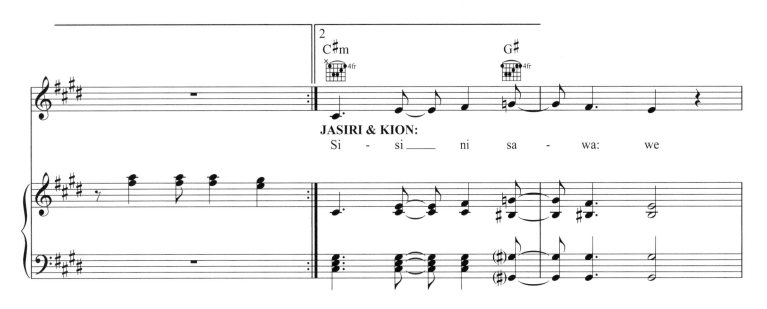

JASIRI & KION:
Si - si ___ ni sa - wa: we

Si - si____ ni sa - wa: we are the ____ same. ____

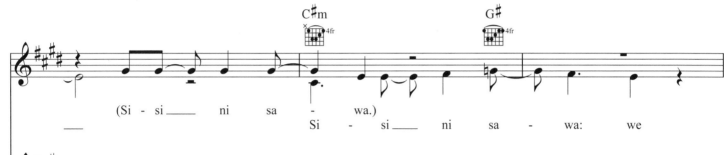

(Si - si____ ni sa - wa.) Si - si____ ni sa - wa: we

are the ____ same. ____ Si - si____ ni sa -

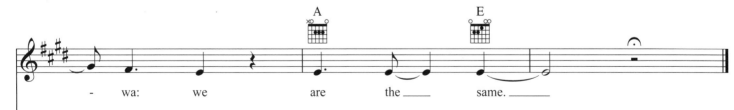

- wa: we are the ____ same. ____

OUTTA THE WAY

Words and Music by BEAU BLACK
and FORD RILEY

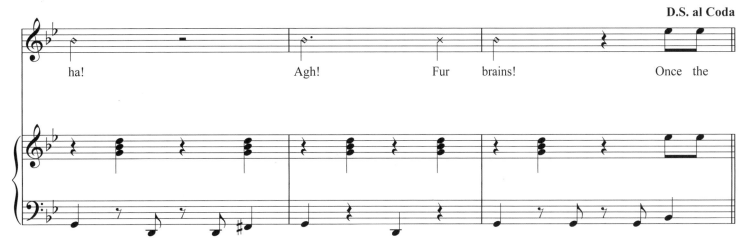

ha!   Agh!   Fur   brains!   Once   the

CODA

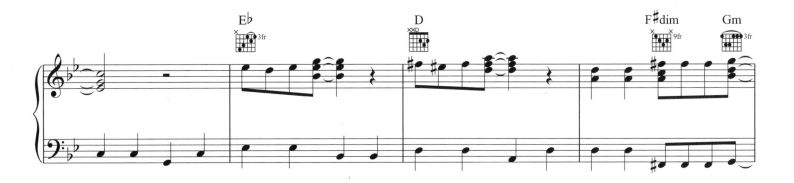

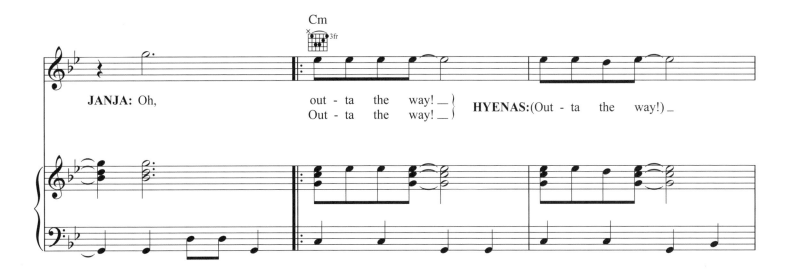

JANJA: Oh,   out - ta   the   way! _\
                  Out - ta   the   way! _   **HYENAS:**(Out - ta   the   way!) _

DUTIES OF THE KING

Words and Music by BEAU BLACK
and FORD RILEY

ZAZU:
Ev-'ry-one in the pride-lands, big or small, looks for-ward to when-ev-er you may call. A vis-it from _ your high-ness is an hon-or, yes, it's true:

62

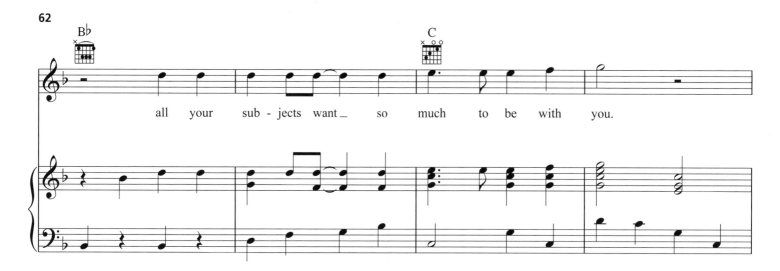

all your sub - jects want _ so much to be with you.

So em - brace your po - si - tion, _

the roy - al tra - di - tion. _

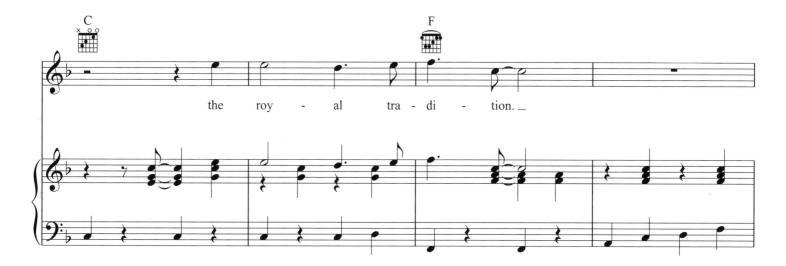

De - light _ in the pride - lands with ev - 'ry lit - tle thing, ___

in all __ of the won-der-ful __ du-ties of __ the king! __

You

wel-come birds __ from all a-round, __ grant ga-zelles __ their graz-ing ground, ap-

prove the of-fi-cial tur-a-co whis-tles, guide the clear-ing of point-y this-tles!

BUNGA THE WISE

Words and Music by BEAU BLACK,
JOHN LOY and FORD RILEY

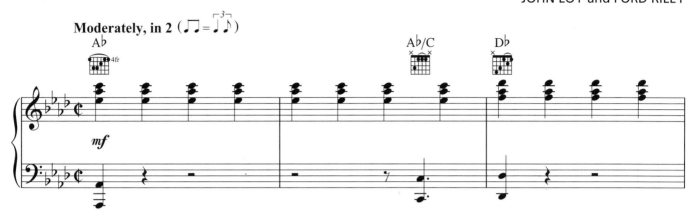

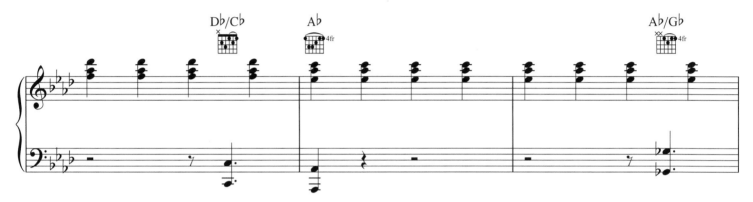

TIMON & PUMBAA: There's one hon-ey bad-ger who's

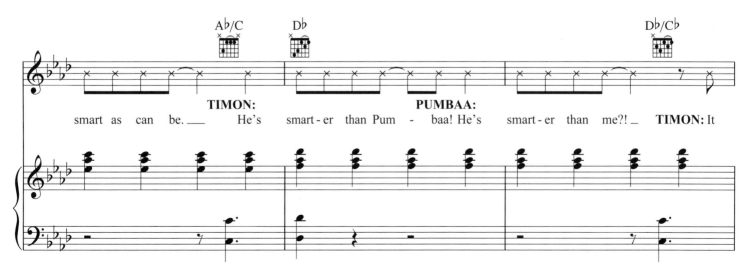

TIMON: smart as can be.___ He's smart-er than Pum - baa! PUMBAA: He's smart-er than me?!___ TIMON: It

MY OWN WAY

Words and Music by BEAU BLACK
and FORD RILEY

and do - ing it on ___ my own. ___ There's noth -
My life is what I ___ make it, ___ and I ___

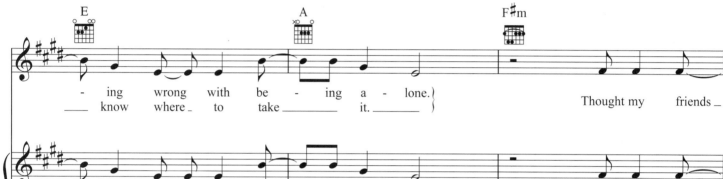

- ing wrong with be - ing a - lone.
___ know where ___ to take ___ it. ___ Thought my friends ___

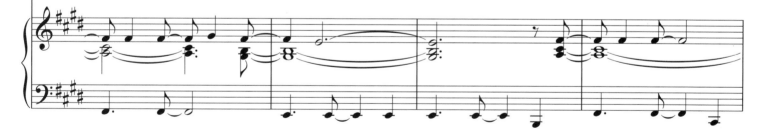

___ al - read - y knew, ___ to ___ my - self ___

I must ___ be true, ___ be true, ___ be true. ___

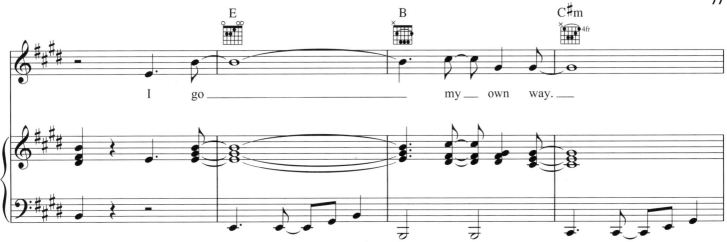

I go _____ my ___ own way. ___

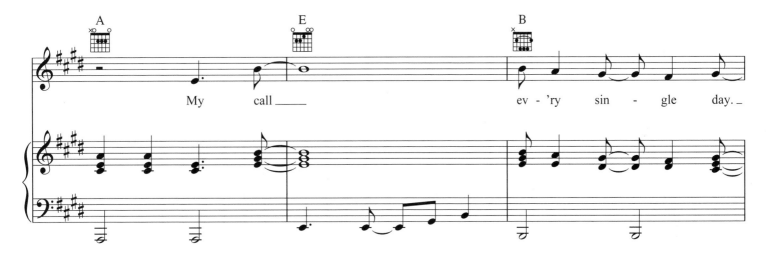

My call _____ ev - 'ry sin - gle day. _

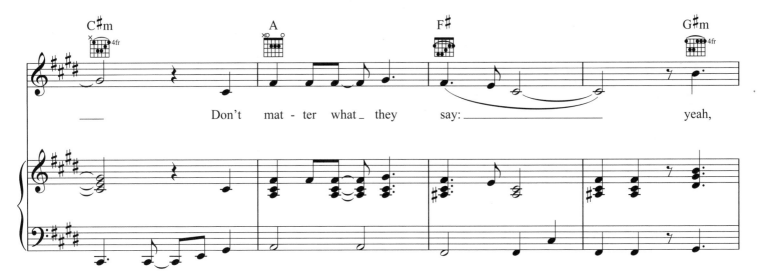

___ Don't mat - ter what _ they say: _____ yeah,

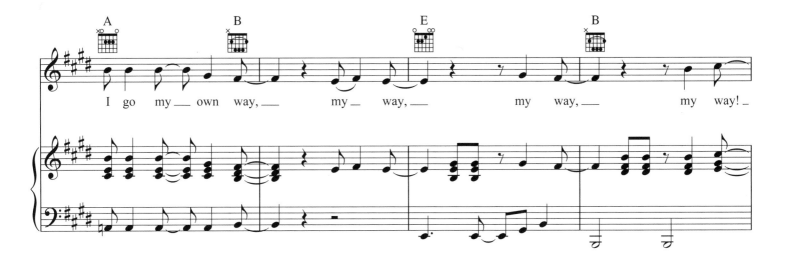

I go my ___ own way, ___ my ___ way, ___ my way, ___ my way! _

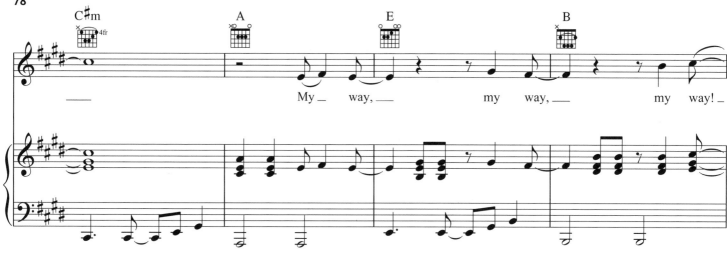

My __ way, __ my way, __ my way! __

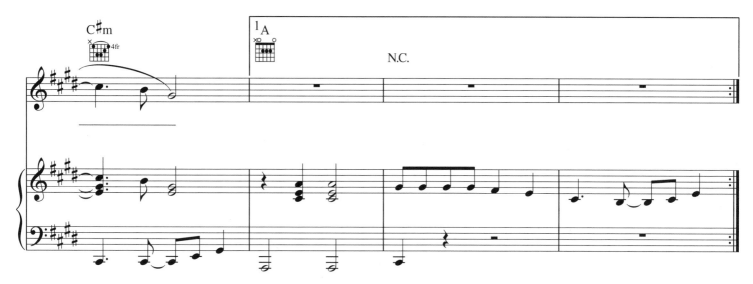

Thought my friends __ al - read - y knew, __

being __ my - self, __ it's what __ I do, __

I do, ____ I do. ____

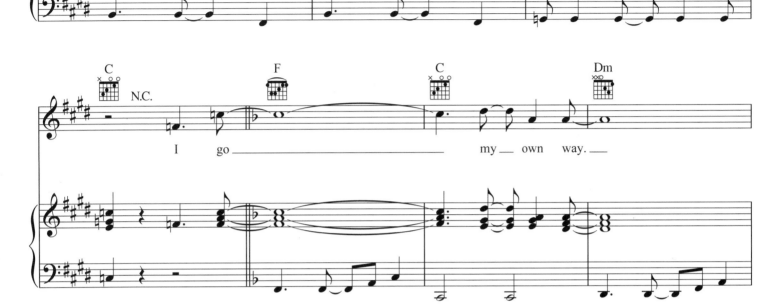

I go _____ my ___ own way. ___

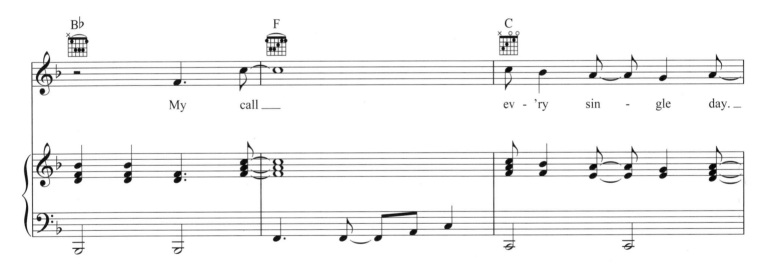

My call ___ ev - 'ry sin - gle day. _

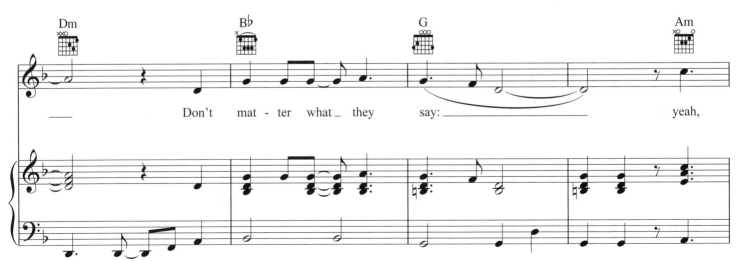

Don't mat - ter what ___ they say: _____ yeah,

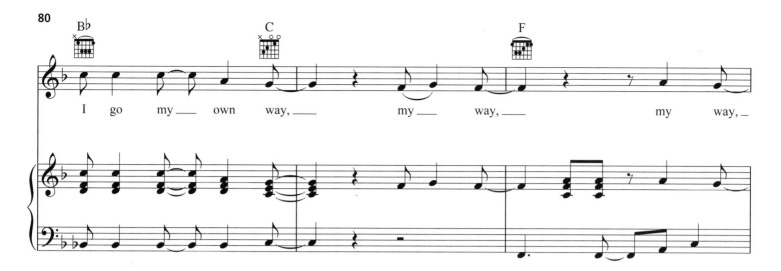

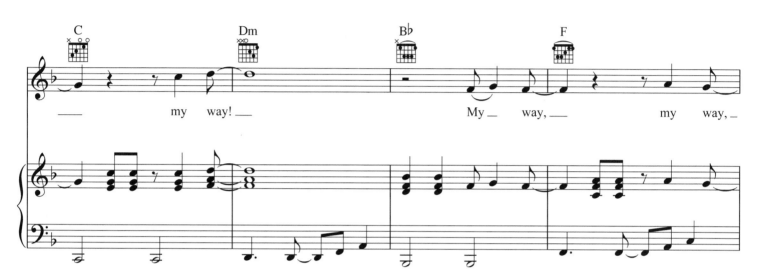

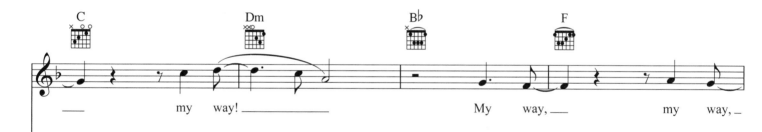

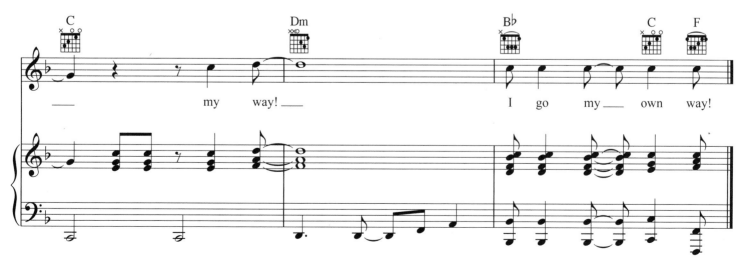

JACKAL STYLE

Words and Music by BEAU BLACK
and FORD RILEY

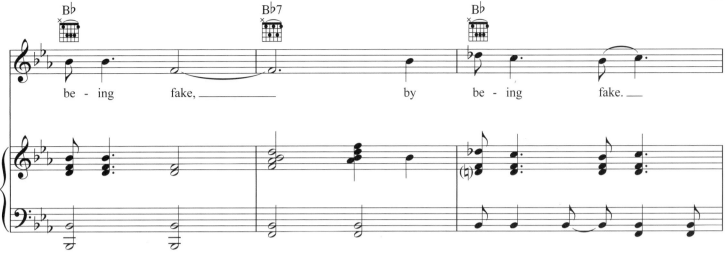

being fake, _____ by being fake. _____

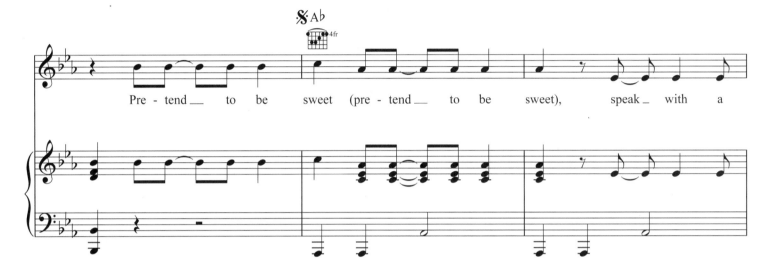

Pre-tend __ to be sweet (pre-tend __ to be sweet), speak __ with a

smile (speak __ with a smile). Then __ you can take things

jack - al style! E - ven if you're mad (e - ven if you're

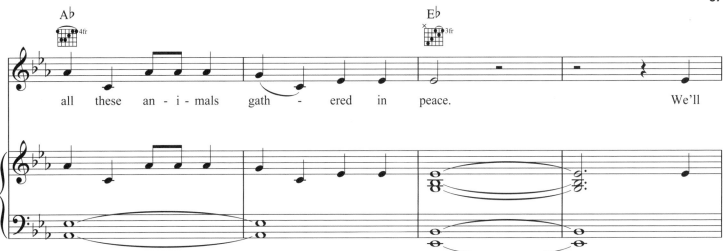

all these an - i - mals gath - ered in peace. We'll

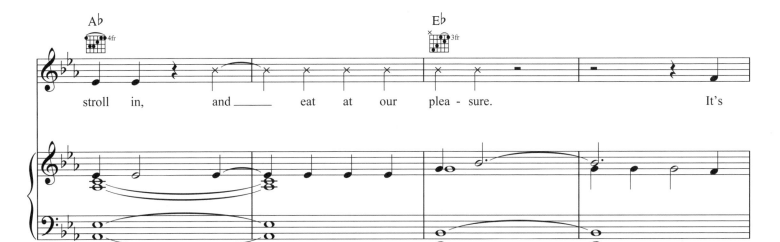

stroll in, and _____ eat at our plea - sure. It's

gon - na be one a - maz - ing feast! _ It's gon - na be one a - maz -

D.S. al Coda

- ing feast! _____ Pre - tend _ to be

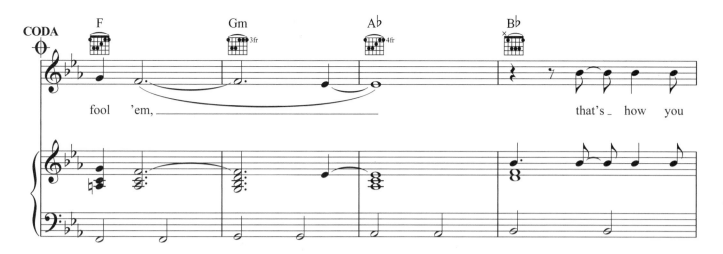

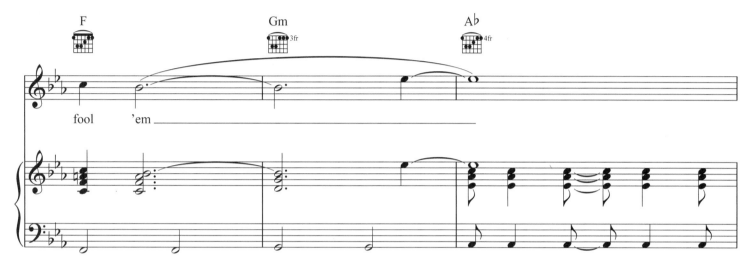

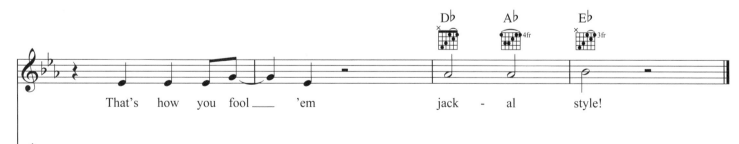

PANIC AND RUN

Words and Music by BEAU BLACK
and FORD RILEY

*Recorded a half step lower.

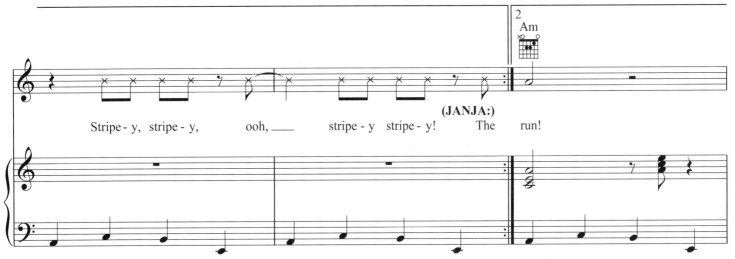

Stripe - y, stripe - y, ooh, ___ stripe - y stripe - y! The run!

(JANJA:)

Ooh, ___ we're gon - na get - cha. Yeah! ___ We're gon - na get - cha!

Get - cha! Get - cha! Pan - ic and run, (Hey!) pan - ic and run. (Oh!)

IT IS TIME

Words and Music by BEAU BLACK
and FORD RILEY

and ev-'ry-one look-ing up to me ___ will see who I was

born to be. ___ It is time. ___ To face ___

___ the world ___ on my own. ___ It is time. ___

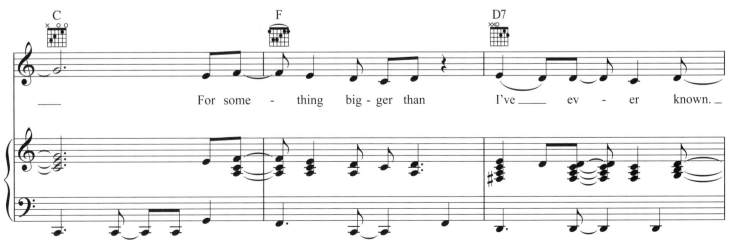

For some - thing big-ger than I've ___ ev - er known. ___